Nature Nurture
(415) 751-40

S0-AVD-173

AMAZING
THINGS
ANIMALS
DO

Published by Maple Tree Press Inc.
51 Front Street East, Suite 200, Toronto, Ontario M5E 1B3

Text © 2003 Marilyn Baillie
Illustrations © 2003 Romi Caron
This book contains material that has previously appeared in *Side by Side: Animals Who Help Each Other* © 1997, *Little Wonders: Animal Babies and Their Families* © 1995, *Time to Eat: Animals Who Hide and Save Their Food* © 1995, *Wild Talk: How Animals Talk to Each Other* © 1996

Distributed in the United States by Firefly Books (U.S.) Inc.
230 Fifth Avenue, Suite 1607, New York, NY 10001

We acknowledge the financial support of the Canada Council for the Arts, the Ontario Arts Council, and the Government of Canada through the Book Publishing Industry Development Program (BPIDP) for our publishing activities.

Consultant
Dr. Katherine E. Wynne-Edwards, PhD, Biology Dept., Queen's University, Kingston, Ontario

Author Acknowledgements
A special thank-you to Dr. Katherine Wynne-Edwards for her expertise and generous assistance. A big thank-you to Publisher Sheba Meland and editor Kat Mototsune for their energy and enthusiasm, to Julia Naimska for her creative design and to Romi Caron for her engaging illustrations.

Dedication
To Cali and Christine and all their animal friends

Cataloguing in Publication Data
Baillie, Marilyn
        Amazing things animals do / written by Marilyn Baillie ; illustrated by Romi Caron.

Consists of 4 works by the author previously published separately: Time to eat, Little wonders, Wild talk, and Side by side.
ISBN 1-894379-57-8

        1. Animal behavior--Juvenile literature. 2. Animals--Juvenile literature. I. Caron, Romi II. Title.

QL751.5.B34 2003   j591.5   C2003-900797-9

Design & art direction: Julia Naimska and Claudia Dávila
Illustrations: Romi Caron

Photo Credits
Page 12: Tui de Roy/Animals Animals; 14, 34: Luiz C. Marigo/Peter Arnold, Inc.; 16, 22: Norbert Wu/Peter Arnold, Inc.; 18: M. & C. Photography/Peter Arnold, Inc.; 20: Stephen J. Krasemann/DRK Photo; 24: Fred Bavendam/Valan Photos; 26: Margot Conte/Animals Animals; 28: John Cancalosi/Peter Arnold, Inc.; 30: Fritz Pölking/Peter Arnold, Inc.; 32: Bill Wood/Bruce Coleman Inc.; 40: African Lion Safari & Game Farm Ltd.; 42: John Cancalosi/Valan Photos; 44: Clem Haagner/Bruce Coleman Inc.; 46: Stephen J. Drasemen/DRK Photo; 48: Merlin D. Tuttle/Bat Conservation International; 50: Marty Cordano/DRK Photo; 52: Kevin Schafer/Mega Press Images; 54 David Smart/DRK Photo; 56: Rudie H. Kuiter/Animals Animals – O.S.F.; 58: Bill Ivy; 60: Margot Conte/Animals Animals; 62: John Markham/Bruce Coleman Inc.; 68: Tom Wiewandt/DRK Photo; 70: Partrige Films/Animals Animals/O.S.F.; 72: Herman H. Giethoorn/Valan Photos; 74: Stephen Pruett-Jones; 76: Dick Haneda; 78 Raymond Mendez/Animals Animals; 80: John Shaw/Bruce Colman Inc.; 82 Stephen J. Krasemann/Valan Photos; 84: Wayne Lankinen/Bruce Coleman Inc.; 86: Ian Murphy/Tony Stone Images; 88: Bill Ivy; 90: J.A. Wilkinson/Valan Photos; 96: Wolfgang Bayer/Bruce Coleman Inc.; 98, 104, 106, 110, 112, 116: J.D. Taylor; 100: Gerard Lacz/Peter Arnold, Inc.; 102: John M. Burnley/Bruce Coleman Inc.; 108: Arthur Strange/Valan Photos; 114: Wayne Lankinen/Valan Photos; 118: J.A. Wilkinson/Valan Photos; 120-127: as above.

Printed in Hong Kong

A   B   C   D   E   F

AMAZING THINGS ANIMALS DO

Marilyn Baillie ✳ art by Romi Caron

MAPLE TREE PRESS

Contents

Contents

Side by Side
Animals Who Help Each Other

HELPING OUT

You live with your family, but there are other very important people in your life, too. Friends and neighbors, teachers and other kids — you help them and they help you. Some animals live side by side with other kinds of animals. They help each other out in surprising ways. Animals can help each other find food or a place to live, or even keep each other safe and healthy. When different animals help each other out, life is a little easier for them.

Animals like the honeyguide bird and the ratel become partners to find and open a beehive. Sometimes many kinds of animals live in the same place and share the food that grows there. This is how giraffes, gerenuks, zebras and gazelles all live together on the African plains.

There are even animals who share their homes. You might find all kinds of animals in the tunnels that prairie dogs dig. How many prairie dogs can you count in this picture? Can you spot another animal who has hopped into a prairie dog burrow to hide? Now turn the page to meet many amazing animals who live side by side.

BIG AND LITTLE

How does a giant Galapagos tortoise get rid of the tiny bugs that latch onto her body? Her broad feet are good for holding up her bathtub-sized shell, but they are too clumsy to scratch at the insects. The jagged edge of her mouth is perfect for tearing up food, but no good for nibbling the annoying ticks that bite her leathery skin. She needs help!

To her rescue come hungry finches. The little birds jump around in front of the tortoise to get her attention. The tortoise tilts her shell up, and stretches her neck out as if to say, "Come aboard." The finches hop onto the tortoise and pick the insects off her skin with their tiny beaks. The ticks make a delicious dinner for them. Finally, when they've eaten all the insects, the birds lift their wings and fly away.

MONKEY BUSINESS

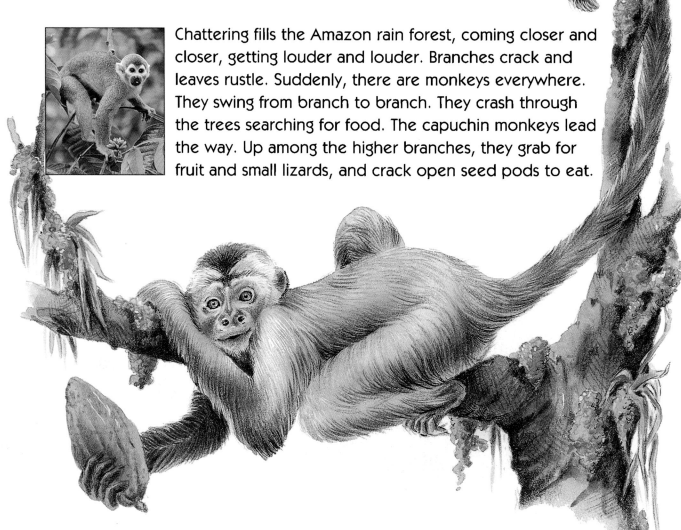

Chattering fills the Amazon rain forest, coming closer and closer, getting louder and louder. Branches crack and leaves rustle. Suddenly, there are monkeys everywhere. They swing from branch to branch. They crash through the trees searching for food. The capuchin monkeys lead the way. Up among the higher branches, they grab for fruit and small lizards, and crack open seed pods to eat.

Smaller squirrel monkeys follow along behind. Hungrily they search the leaves for leftovers the capuchins drop. They find and eat insects that have been shaken out of their hiding places. And the more monkeys there are travelling together, the more eyes there are to watch for danger. If one monkey spots the shadow of an eagle, it gives a sharp cry of warning. Suddenly, all the monkeys will hide, leaving the rain forest still and quiet. But soon it will be safe again, and the monkeys will go on their noisy way.

CATCH A RIDE

A shark glides through the ocean. He will attack and eat almost anything. But does he know a special kind of fish is attached to his body? Fish called remoras stick to the shark using the strong suckers on top of their heads. They ride along, waiting for the shark to find something to eat. The shark eats by tearing at his food with his teeth, and the remoras let go to eat the floating scraps he misses.

When the shark is ready to travel again, the remoras grasp on. They cling to the shark's body, eating the small creatures that live on his skin. The remoras move their suckers along the shark's skin, scraping tiny mites into their open mouths. The remoras keep the shark clean and healthy. In return, the remoras get all the mites and fish scraps they need to eat, and a free ride through the sea.

PROTECTOR ANTS

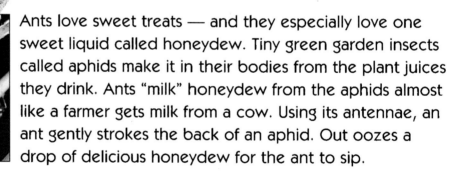

Ants love sweet treats — and they especially love one sweet liquid called honeydew. Tiny green garden insects called aphids make it in their bodies from the plant juices they drink. Ants "milk" honeydew from the aphids almost like a farmer gets milk from a cow. Using its antennae, an ant gently strokes the back of an aphid. Out oozes a drop of delicious honeydew for the ant to sip.

Sometimes ants keep herds of aphids. The ants protect the aphids and care for them. Some ants carry their aphids, one by one, to places where there are good plants to eat. Other ants make tiny mud shelters to protect their aphids from the weather. And some keep their aphids safe in the ant nest at night. Ants that store aphid eggs over the winter are sure to have a new batch of aphids to milk in the spring. And if a hungry ladybug comes looking for aphids to eat, the ants attack it and chase it away.

RHINO ALARM

A rhinoceros and her calf wander from bush to bush, nibbling on branch tips. The huge mother seems calm, but most animals keep their distance from her. Rhinos have sudden tempers, and can attack in an instant. With a swift turn, this mother rhino will charge anything she thinks might threaten her baby. But she doesn't seem to mind the egrets hopping and bobbing at her feet.

As the rhinos walk through the grass, their lumbering feet stir up insects. A surprised grasshopper pops up into the air. Snatch! A waiting egret snaps it up. The egret can find all kinds of insects to eat, including the ticks that live on the rhino's rubbery skin. The egret's sharp eyes also help the rhino mother protect her baby. The egret can spot danger — a hungry hyena — long before the short-sighted rhino mother sees it. The egret flaps its wings, alerting the rhino to keep her baby safe at her side.

Hanging Around

A sloth hangs upside down in a tree. Silent and still, she is hard to spot in the dappled shadows of the rain forest. She moves in slow motion along the branch, drowsily reaching for a leaf to taste. Her baby dozes, cradled by its mother's tummy. Sloths almost never leave the high branches at the tops of the trees. They slowly climb down only to leave their droppings in the ground.

Sloths are so slow, they can be a shelter for smaller animals. Each hair in the sloth's fur is covered with very small scales. Tiny, plantlike creatures called algae live under these scales. The algae make the sloth's fur a greenish color, blending the sloth and her baby into the leafy treetops. Not even a sharp-eyed eagle or hungry jaguar can see them dangling there.

Tiny moths also make their home in the sloth's shaggy coat. Female moths lay eggs in the sloth's droppings. There the eggs become caterpillars and finally change to adult moths. Up into the trees the moths fly, to find homes in the fur of other sloths. Meanwhile, not noticing the algae and moths living on them, the sloth and her baby sleep the day away. Zzzzz.

FISHY FRIENDS

The sea anemone waves its stinging tentacles in the warm tropical sea. Fish that brush against the tips of the bright arms are stunned by the poison there, and are pulled into the anemone's mouth to be eaten. But two clown fish safely dart in and out, around the anemone. They eat the floating bits left over from the anemone's meal. They even live among the poisonous tentacles.

Why are the clown fish not harmed? When they were young, these clown fish chose this sea anemone to live with. The clown fish brushed lightly against the tentacles. Then they quickly pulled away. They rubbed against the stingers again and again, gradually getting used to the poison. In time, they were able to dive into the tentacles and live there. Safe from other fish that might eat them, the clown fish help the anemone, too. Their bright colors attract larger fish looking for a meal. Before they can eat the clown fish, the anemone stings the hunters. They become a meal that the anemone shares with the clown fish.

UNDERGROUND TOWN

The prairie might look deserted from above, but there's a whole town under the ground — a prairie dog town. Hundreds of prairie dogs dig deep into the prairie soil, making dens to live in and tunnels to connect them. They dig lots of burrows — more than they need to live in. So other animals live there too. Snakes sleep through the winter in some dens. Small animals — mice or rabbits — sometimes dart into a tunnel to escape a hunting coyote. Prairie dogs don't seem to mind having neighbors.

Even birds live here. A burrowing owl laid her eggs in an empty prairie dog hole to keep them safe. Her mate keeps watch above ground. The owls could dig their own burrow if they had to. But they found a ready-made tunnel, with the grass around the entrance clipped short by hungry prairie dogs. In the short grass, it's easier for the owl to hunt for grasshoppers and mice. It's easier for him to spot danger at a distance.

At the first sign of danger — a hawk's shadow or the sight of a ferret — a prairie dog will bark, "chirk, chirk!" Then it will shriek a sharp alarm. Others will repeat the warning whistle. In a flash, the owl and prairie dogs will dive into safe burrows. Then all there will be to see above the ground is the golden grass waving in the soft prairie breeze.

ROOMMATES

The petrel spends months fishing for food away from her home. But finally, she returns to her nest in the side of a cliff. Now she will rest and lay her eggs. But what's this? Two eyes shine from inside her hole in the cliff wall. A tuatara has moved in while she was gone. The petrel doesn't chase away the intruder, but settles into her nest with the tuatara as a roommate.

It might seem awfully crowded, but the roommates don't spend a lot of time under the same roof. The tuatara hunts at night and the petrel fishes during the day. The tuatara eats all the bothersome insects in the petrel's nest. It might eat eggs and baby birds from other nests, but not from the nest it shares with the petrel. When the petrel flies out to fish, the tuatara stays behind and keeps the house clean.

GRASSLAND NEIGHBORS

The wide African plain spreads as far as the eye can see. Acacia trees reach up from the vast stretches of grass. You might not think the leaves and grasses found on the plain would provide enough food for many animals to eat. But thousands of animals all graze here — giraffes and gerenuks, zebras and gazelles. They share the food by eating different parts of the plants.

Up, up, the giraffe stretches her neck. Her tough upper lip and long tongue curl around twigs and leaves at the very top of the acacia tree. No other animal can reach so high. At another tree, gerenuks nibble on lower branches. The branches are still too high for most animals to reach. But the gerenuks can balance on their hind legs to get at the leaves and shoots.

Grazing animals share the grasses of the open plains — zebras and Thomson's gazelles all together. The zebras eat the tender tops of the taller grasses. The gazelles get enough food in the shorter, coarser grasses left behind. And if any animal spots a hunting lioness, it gives an alarm that starts hundreds of them all running for safety.

SHINY CLEAN

All kinds of fish live in the coral reef. They swim around, making the ocean bright with flashes of fins and tails. But some fish aren't going anywhere. What are they waiting for? This is a cleaning station in the ocean, like a car wash for your car. Tiny cleaner wrasse fish are on the job. A rainbow of little butterflyfish all wait their turn to be cleaned one by one.

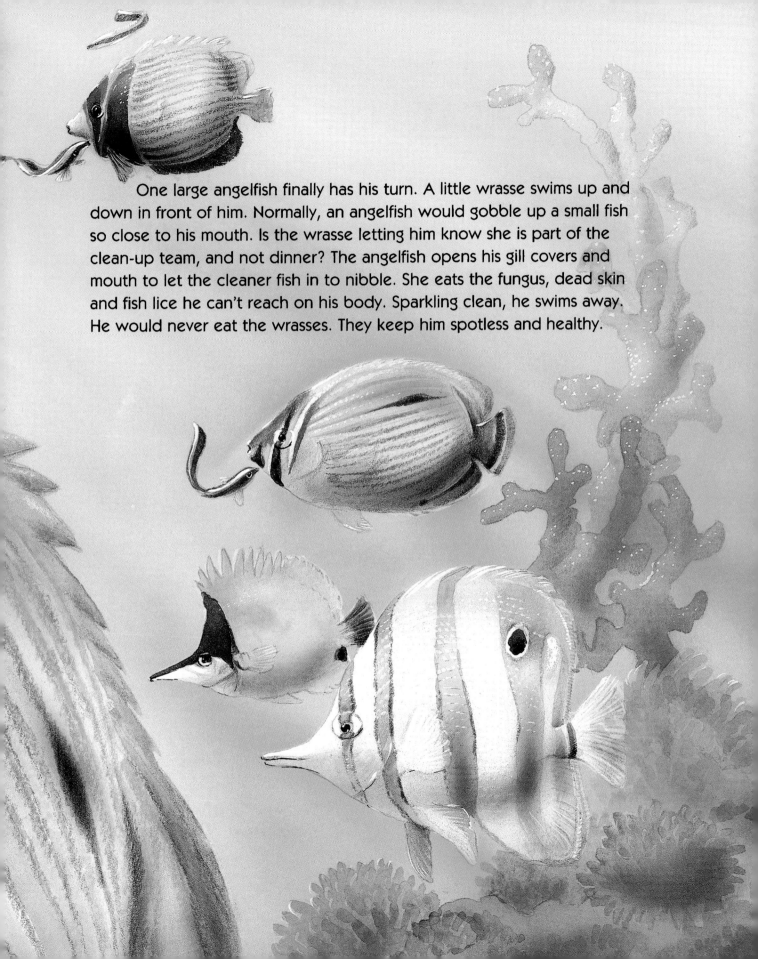

One large angelfish finally has his turn. A little wrasse swims up and down in front of him. Normally, an angelfish would gobble up a small fish so close to his mouth. Is the wrasse letting him know she is part of the clean-up team, and not dinner? The angelfish opens his gill covers and mouth to let the cleaner fish in to nibble. She eats the fungus, dead skin and fish lice he can't reach on his body. Sparkling clean, he swims away. He would never eat the wrasses. They keep him spotless and healthy.

TREAT FOR TWO

The honeyguide calls as she flies, dipping and swooping. Her tail fans out, showing off the white feathers. On the ground, a furry companion follows along. The ratel growls softly, as together they head for a honeybee nest. The honeyguide loves to eat beeswax and the grubs that will grow up into bees. The ratel eats insects, plants, small animals and fruit — but honey is a special treat.

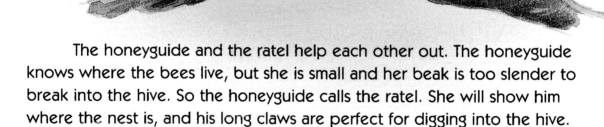

The honeyguide and the ratel help each other out. The honeyguide knows where the bees live, but she is small and her beak is too slender to break into the hive. So the honeyguide calls the ratel. She will show him where the nest is, and his long claws are perfect for digging into the hive.

The bird's song changes as she leads the ratel to where the nest is hidden in a hollow tree. He rubs the smelly scent from under his tail all over the nest opening. The smell stuns the bees so they cannot sting. Then the ratel can rip into the nest, and the honeyguide joins in. Mmmm, sweet honey and delicious bee grubs!

Little Wonders

Animal Babies and Their Families

BRINGING UP BABY

Can you remember when you were a baby? You couldn't do things for yourself, so your family looked after you, day and night. They kept you warm and safe. They fed you and helped you learn how to talk and how to walk. Many animal babies need the same kind of special care. Some of them hatch from eggs. Others are born alive, and drink their mother's milk. There are animals that look after themselves from the moment they are born, but many animal babies need families to care for them, just like you.

There are all kinds of animal families. Baby elephants and meerkats live in big family groups. Sea otter mothers and seahorse fathers look after their young by themselves. And cuckoo chicks are raised by birds that are not even cuckoos!

Animal babies come in ones, or twos, or more! Bats and orangutans have one baby at a time. Baby polar bears are often born as twins. And some animals have many babies at once. How many baby alligators can you count in this picture? Now, let's meet some special animal babies and their amazing families.

BIG BABY

What's all the excitement in the elephant herd? A baby has been born! To welcome the calf, the elephants stroke him with their trunks and rumble deep in their throats. Just hours after he is born, the calf stands up to take his first wobbly step. Soon the elephants will be on the move again. With gentle trunks and feet to nudge him along, the calf will be able to keep up with the herd.

There are no full grown male elephants here, since they live on their own. The herd is a family of female elephants and their young, all related to this littlest calf. Covered in dust from their journey, they linger under a shady tree. The thirsty calf drinks his mother's milk. She will feed him for about two years, but the herd will help her guard and protect him. One young female will become a baby-sitter, for times when the baby's mother is busy eating. The baby-sitter will help teach him to use his trunk to drink and grab food. She'll play with him in the cool water of the watering hole, and even show him how to squirt showers of water over himself. Whoosh!

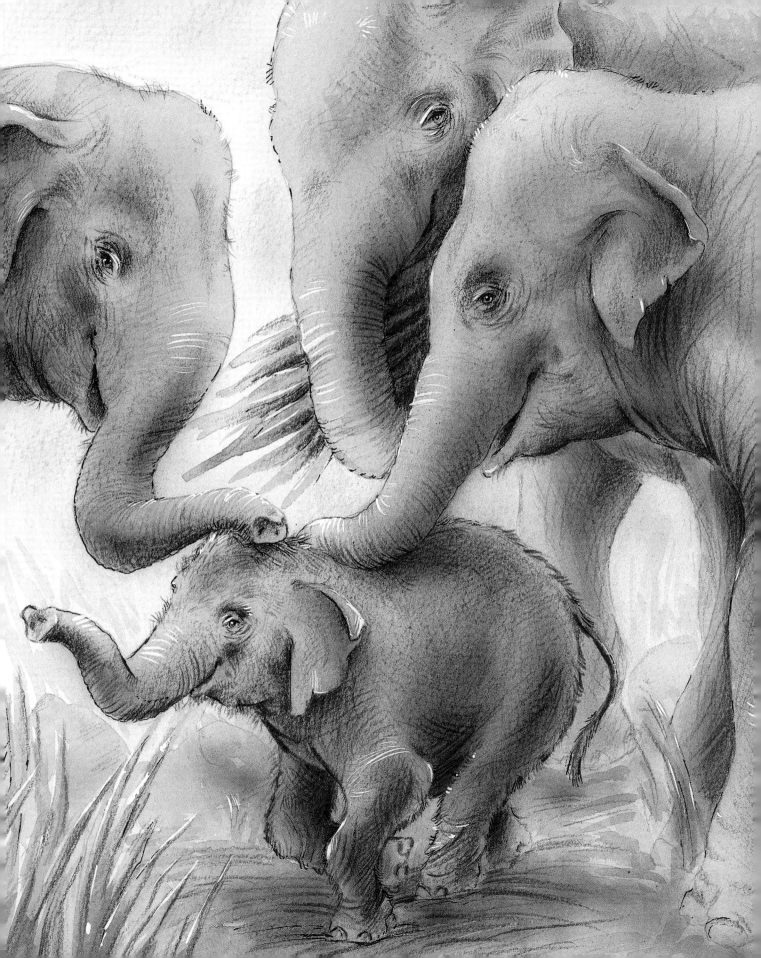

POUCH HOUSE

Who's that hiding in a pocket? It's a young kangaroo, or joey, peering out of the furry pouch on his mother's belly. At nine months old, he spends much of his time outside the pouch. But when he is startled or sleepy, he is safest in here. Soon the joey will leave the pouch for good. But he'll still poke his head inside to drink the milk that is just right for a kangaroo his age.

Hidden deep in the pouch is a surprise. Another baby! A newborn sister shares the mother kangaroo's cozy pocket. Naked and tiny, she has climbed from the birth opening into the pouch, just as her older brother did nine months ago. She clings tightly and suckles her mother's milk. This milk is different from the milk her brother drinks, and contains everything a newborn needs to grow. She drinks and snoozes, and doesn't mind when — flip — her brother somersaults right into the pouch beside her!

SAFE INSIDE

A long, red beak pokes out of a hole in an old tree. The red-billed hornbill has found a perfect place to nest. She has a special way to keep safe in this secret hideaway. The hornbill and her mate mix mud with their bills. They smear it over the opening in the tree. She plasters from the inside and he builds on the outside. In no time she is walled up in the nest and can lay her eggs in safety.

There is a small hole left in the wall, just big enough for a hornbill's beak. The male passes food through the hole to his mate and the chicks that hatch from the eggs. The father hornbill is kept busy feeding his whole family, and soon he needs help. The mother hornbill pecks at the dried mud covering the hole. Crack! The wall breaks open and out she flies. The baby birds plaster themselves in again, sticking up broken pieces of the wall with their beaks. Now both parents can gather food for the quickly growing nestlings. They push fruit and insects into the hole, and the chicks eat until they are big enough to break out and fly off on their own.

ROCK-A-BYE BABY

Back and forth, a mother sea otter and her baby rock in the ocean waves. She holds her pup close against the soft fur of her stomach. She nuzzles and cuddles him, gently grooming his fur to keep it clean and waterproof. The pup drinks his mother's rich, sweet milk. It's just the food he needs to keep warm and grow in the cold ocean water. The baby sea otter was born here in the ocean. Mother and baby live in the kelp beds, a thick forest of seaweed. They float just offshore, among the strands of kelp waving in the tides.

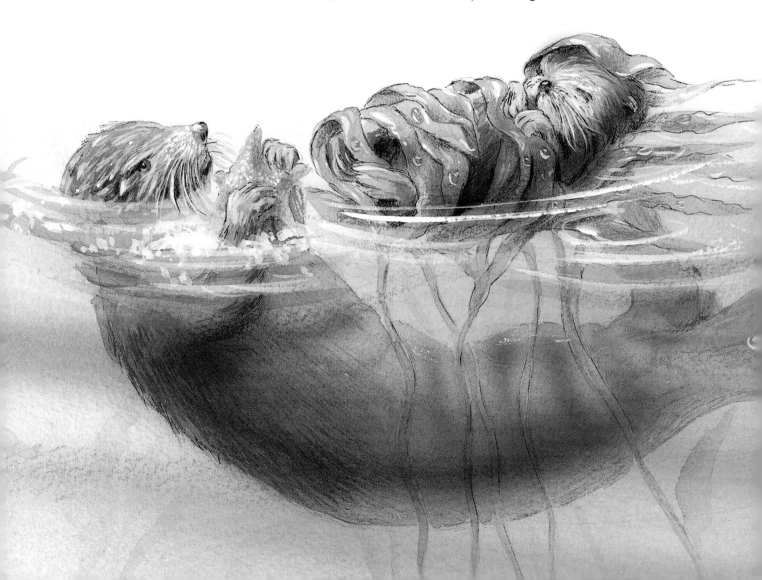

Soon this pup will be ready to learn about life in the sea. His mother will teach him how to swim and dive. She will show him how to find shell-fish and sea urchins on the ocean floor. He'll learn to crack them open against a sharp rock to get at the tender meat inside. In a year, he will be ready to leave his mother and live with the others in the kelp.

But for now, his mother takes complete care of him. She makes sure he is safe, even when she has to dive for her dinner. Around and around her baby she wraps a strand of kelp. She doesn't want him to drift away while she is gone. The air bubbles in the kelp will help to keep him warm. He waits for her return, safe and warm in his ocean cradle.

UPSIDE-DOWN NURSERY

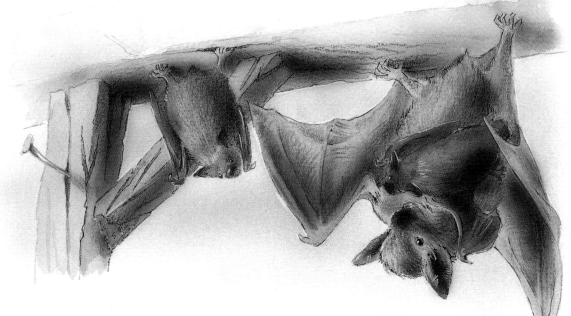

 Flap, flap, whir-r-r-r! Little brown bats swoop out into the summer dusk. Shadows shaped like winged mice cross the sky. These bats are mother bats, living together in an old, empty barn. Hanging from the ceiling, each one gives birth to a single pup. The newborn bats hold tightly to their mothers for the first day or so, clutching their fur and drinking their milk. But baby bats grow quickly. After a few days, the mother bats leave the barn nursery to hunt for food. They need to eat a lot of insects to have enough milk for their pups.

Back in the barn, hundreds of pups bunch together for warmth. They cling to the wooden beams with their curved claws, dangling upside-down from the ceiling. As each mother returns, she calls to her baby and listens for an answer. She makes her way through the throng of squeaking young, following her baby's voice. Other pups try to snatch some milk, but she pushes them away. She can tell by smell which pup is her very own. She draws it close to feed it, hanging in the nursery high above the barn floor.

SWAMP BABIES

 Reptile babies are born all set to survive on their own, so most reptile parents don't stay around to care for their young. But alligators are different. First, a mother alligator makes a big nest by piling plants and sand at the side of the marsh. She lays about forty white eggs in the nest and then covers them. Nearby, she waits and waits for the first little cry.

"Reak, reak!" The tiny alligators squeak as they struggle to break out of their shells. Their mother hears them, and rushes to the nest. She rips it open to help them climb out. She gently scoops some of the babies into her huge mouth and carries them to the water. Other tiny ones waddle behind her as she calls to them. The babies can already swim, and they search for snails and bugs to eat. Their mother doesn't need to teach them a thing about life in the sunny swamp. But she is there to protect them. A baby chirps a warning and they all dive for cover. The mother alligator hisses and lunges at a raccoon crouching in the tall grass. Her ferocious mouth is enough to frighten anything away!

PENGUIN DAYCARE

Icy winter winds whistle around the South Pole. All through the dark polar winter, male emperor penguins stand in blizzards of snow. For weeks they don't eat and they move very carefully. Each bird is protecting an egg propped on top of his feet. The female penguin lays her egg, and then shuffles to the sea to fish and eat. To keep the egg from freezing on the bare ice, the father penguin balances it on his flipper feet until it hatches. The egg is tucked under a fold of skin, warm and safe in his soft front feathers.

Finally, a fluffy chick breaks out of the egg. She nestles in her father's feathers, and peeks over his feet. The mother penguin returns in the spring to take care of the chick. Now the hungry father can go fishing. As the growing chick needs more and more food, both parents leave her to fish together for their baby. But the little chick is never lonely. She stays and plays in a penguin nursery with hundreds of other chicks. There are always some adult penguins around to keep the chicks warm in the cold spring air, and safe from animals that would like to eat them. But listen! The chick hears her parents' loud whistles. She pushes through the squawking crowd of chicks, whistling back. A fish feast is on its way!

TREETOP TRAVELLER

High in the leafy rain forest, an orangutan searches for her favorite fruit. She swings gracefully from branch to branch, weaving her way through the dappled treetops. Clinging to her fur, close against her side is her baby. He was born a year ago, tiny and helpless. Now he is big enough to explore a little on his own, but he still needs his mother's help to get from tree to tree.

For two years the little orangutan will cling to his mother for milk and safety. She'll teach him where to find fruit and how to get around. Little by little he will learn to survive in the forest. Even though young orangutans are very smart, it will be eight years before he is ready to live alone.

As the sun sinks behind the trees, the orangutan mother prepares a nest. High in a tree, she breaks branches and pats them down to make a floor. She makes a roof of big leaves, in case it rains during the night. A bent branch becomes a bridge, so her baby can cross over between the trees. Safe in the treetops, they curl up together for the night.

FATHER'S DAY

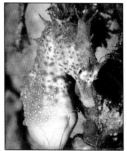
A little fish that has a head like a horse and a tail like a monkey swims slowly through the warm tropical sea. It's a seahorse carrying babies in a bulging pouch, and they're almost ready to be born. But this is not a seahorse mother. It's the male seahorse that guards the babies in his own body. Here they grow until they are ready to be born and swim free.

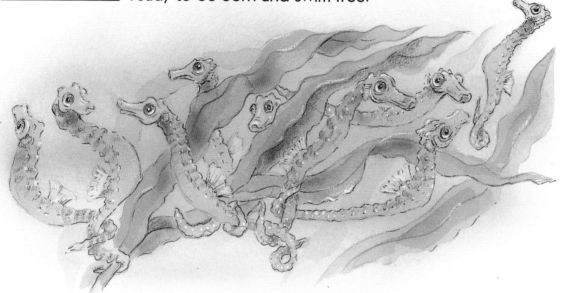

Whoosh! The first baby seahorse pops out of his father's pouch into the water. One, two, three, four . . . many more babies wiggle free. Some cling to each other with their curly tails. Others grasp waving blades of grass. Soon the sea is filled with hundreds of babies from the same pouch. Tiny versions of adult seahorses, they can look after themselves from the moment they are born. Up, up the newborn fish rise to gulp some air at the water's surface. The air fills their swim bladders, so that they can swim better. They search among the seaweed for small shrimp and other bits of seafood to eat, and in a year the babies will be as big as their dad.

BABY-SITTING TIME

A young male meerkat stands on guard. He sniffs the air for the scent of a fox. He scans the desert sand for the shadow of an eagle's wing. When he's sure that there is no danger nearby, a soft chirp and purr from him tells the others, "It's safe." Out of an old termite's nest tumble five playful meerkat kits. Their baby-sitter, a young female, is right at their side. She plays with them and grooms them. The kits suckle milk from her. Some day she might have her own babies. But for now she is much too busy baby-sitting.

When the rest of the meerkats return from the hunt, they bring food to share — beetles, snakes and scorpions. Soon the babies will be too big for just milk, and the hunters will let them take tidbits from their mouths. The adult meerkats all play with the babies, rolling and digging in the dry sand. Then they all snuggle together to sleep. Only the leaders of this close group can have babies. The others help out by hunting for food, keeping watch and caring for the kits. The five babies are looked after by a dozen adult meerkats — their mother, their father and the whole family.

BEAR HUGS

The female polar bear digs a hole in the snow. Her den faces the winter sun to catch its faint warmth. Inside, she gives birth to twins. The two newborn cubs are tiny and completely helpless. Their eyes are closed and they are almost naked. The mother bear ate enough in the fall to last through the winter, and the milk she gives them is rich and creamy enough to keep them warm.

In early spring, the bear cubs are big enough to leave the den and explore. At two months old, they look like playful puppies. They are wide-eyed and covered in thick, fluffy, white fur. The twins tumble out into the spring sunshine. Their mother is hungry after the long winter, and wants to hunt for seals. She nudges them along in the deep snow with her nose, heading towards the open sea. Soon she will begin teaching them how to hunt seals to eat and how to swim. After two years of lessons with their mother, the twins will be ready to live in this wintry world all on their own.

QUICK SWITCH

It's feeding time for baby birds! Crammed in the snug nest is a big cuckoo chick. His beak is wide open and he's very hungry. Mother and father birds fetch worms, caterpillars and flies to feed him. They protect and care for him, even though he is not their chick. They aren't even cuckoo birds! Like foster parents, they are raising someone else's baby that has been left in their care.

Some female cuckoos don't make nests or raise their babies. They find other birds, large and small, to hatch their eggs and care for their chicks. The cuckoo waits patiently by the nest of another bird. When the nesting mother leaves, the cuckoo swoops in, removes an egg and lays her own in its place. She flies off, knowing that her baby will be raised well.

When the other bird returns to her nest, she doesn't notice anything different about the new egg. She sees that there is the right number of eggs to sit on and hatch. The cuckoo egg hatches first, and the cuckoo is the biggest and hungriest of all the chicks in the nest. Even so, the foster parents feed and care for the cuckoo baby as if it were their own.

Time to Eat

Animals Who Hide and Save Their Food

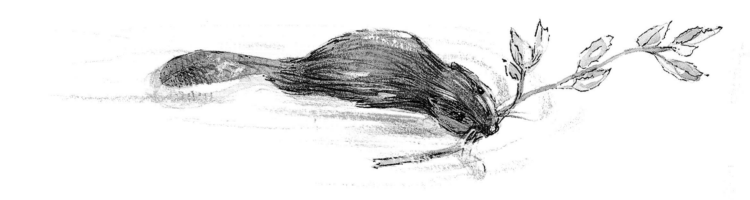

HIDE AND FIND

We keep our food in cupboards and refrigerators. Animals all over the world store and save their food, too. Animals hide and save food for times when they will really need it. They keep meals ready to eat when food can't be found. Some creatures use many hiding places, and others put all their food in one place. Animals sometimes hide food to keep it safe from scavengers, other animals that like to steal a free meal.

Have you ever wrapped a sandwich to keep it fresh until lunchtime? The garden spider wraps silken threads around a bug to save it for later. The great horned owl doesn't need a freezer for its dinner, or an oven to thaw it. It uses cold winter air and the heat from its own body.

We keep forgetting where we put the ketchup! But little birds called chickadees hide hundreds of tiny seeds, and know exactly where to find each one again. The chickadees here have plucked and hidden lots of seeds to eat later. How many seeds can you see? Now, turn the page to meet more animals that store and save their food in amazing ways.

BIG CHEEKS

Daytime is scorching in the desert, but night brings the cool and dark. Once the sun sets, the kangaroo rat hops warily from beneath the sand and scrub to gather seeds. Using her front paws, she neatly packs the seeds into her cheek pockets. Bigger and bigger her cheeks bulge with food. Then . . . hop, hop, the kangaroo rat disappears into her burrow.

The kangaroo rat hurries down deep underground to her nest. There she turns her cheek pockets inside out to empty out every last seed. She sorts the seeds into piles — the small seeds here, the big ones there. Then she hops back into the night for another load.

Soon the desert will get hotter and drier. But the kangaroo rat can stay cool day after day in her underground nest. She won't need to go out for food and water. Her stored seeds give her all the food and liquid she needs. When the hottest season passes, she will leave her burrow again, to gather and hide away seeds.

Safe Acorns

Rat-a-tat-tat! What's that sound? An acorn woodpecker is pecking a hole in a hollow tree. Back and forth bobs his head as he chisels with his long, strong beak. Another woodpecker comes to take her turn at the hole. Then a third one arrives. They take turns pecking and tapping, hammering and rapping at the tree trunk until the hole is just the right size and shape.

A woodpecker flies up with an acorn it has plucked from an oak tree. It stuffs it into the new hole. Hundreds of acorns dot the tree, snug in the notches the woodpeckers have made. If any of the acorns dry up and shrink, the woodpeckers pull them out and wedge them into smaller holes made to fit.

There is enough food here for this woodpecker family group to eat all through the bad weather when food is hard to find. The acorns fit tightly in the holes. Only the sharp-beaked woodpeckers can pry the precious food out. These birds jealously guard their acorns. Any animal who tries to snatch one gets shooed away!

BUG BUNDLE

Look in the raspberry bushes — there's a garden spider on her lacy web. Woven between the stems like a net, the long silk strands of the web have trapped a fly for the spider to eat. The garden spider is spinning her silk. She bundles up the tasty fly in the strong thin threads. She will save this wrapped-up meal for later, dangling the bug bundle from a long strand attached to the web.

How does the spider catch her food? Let's watch and see. Here comes a grasshopper. Thud! It bumps into the web and gets stuck on the sticky silk. Its wiggling makes the web shake, so the spider knows another meal has arrived. The spider picks her way across the web on special threads that are not sticky. She bites her prey to make it hold still while she wraps her silk around it and hangs it up. Then she fixes her web and hangs upside-down near the center, waiting for the next insect to come by.

But her silk-wrapped meals are not always safe. The male garden spider is smaller than she is, and he's a clever thief. He patiently waits on a nearby leaf while the female spider traps and wraps her prey. Then he sneaks up and snips his free meal from the web. He slowly lowers the bundle to the ground on a hanging thread, and carries it away!

Handy Snacks

Fresh figs and other fruits fill the tree branches. But here's a mystery — these fruits didn't grow on these trees. Who put all this fruit here? It was the MacGregor's bowerbird. He has propped juicy fruits in the forks of tree branches, keeping it handy and ready to eat. It's mating season and he has a lot of work to do — no time to fly around and look for food.

The bowerbird piles and fits bits of twigs together around a sapling. Slowly, a tall tower shape grows. He carefully lays a covering of soft moss around the bottom. This is not a nest he's building. It's called a bower, and it's a special place for him to show off to a female bird.

When the bower is finished and he has filled the trees with fresh fruit, the bowerbird is ready. He sees a female bird, and starts to dance around his bower on the moss. Look at his bright orange crest! What a beautiful bower! Surely a new mate will want to come and stay a while?

Up a Tree

The quiet of the African plain is hardly broken by the crack of a branch. In the faint evening light, a spotted shadow slips to the ground from an acacia tree. It's a leopard. She slinks towards a grazing herd of gazelles, and then she pauses, still and silent. Suddenly, with one swift pounce, the leopard catches her supper. The rest of the gazelles bound away.

A pack of hyenas lurks in the grass, watching the leopard eat her supper and hoping to steal the leftovers. She can't keep these scavengers away all by herself. How will she protect the rest of her food?

The leopard grasps the gazelle with her strong jaws and drags the heavy load to a tree. Her sharp claws dig deep into the tree trunk as she hauls up her catch. The leopard slings her food over a sturdy tree branch safe from the hyenas, who can't climb. Then she stretches out on a nearby limb to catnap and keep watch. Now, who would dare steal food from the mighty leopard?

HANGING HONEYPOTS

Home, sweet home for honeypot ants is this nest under the ground. What are those roly-poly balls on the ceiling? The balls are special honeypot ants, puffed up to about eight times their usual size! Each ant is full of stored plant nectar and honeydew, like a balloon filled with sugary water. The storage ants can't move much, so worker ants bring them food and keep them full to bursting.

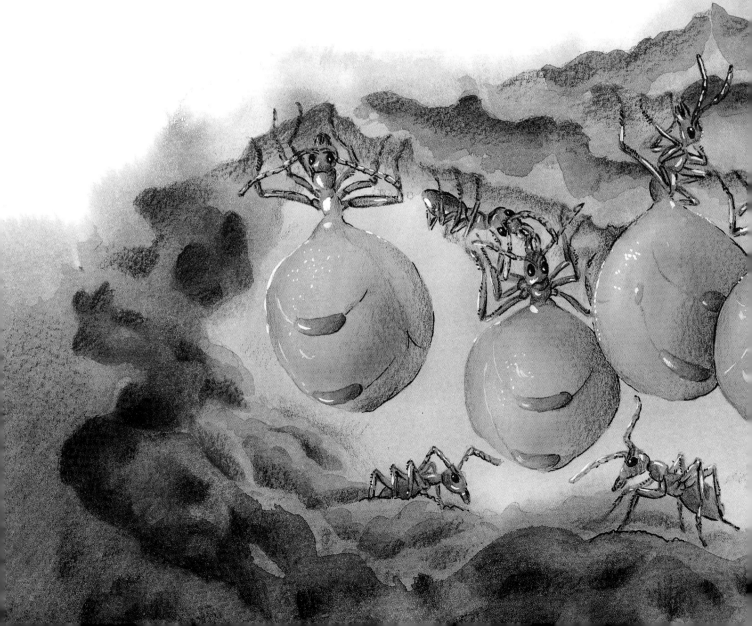

During the dry season, plants wither. There is no nectar in the plants for the worker ants to eat. That's when they get food from their roly-poly friends. Gently they stroke the storage ants with their antennae. The storage ants drop liquid food from their mouths for the hungry workers to sip. The whole nest can live for many months through a dry spell, all thanks to the honeypot storage ants.

COOL TREATS

Far above the ground, the great horned owl sits still as the cold night air. Suddenly — whir-r-r-r! — his wide wings softly cut through the darkness. He swoops down, following a mouse running across the frozen meadow. He snatches the mouse with his needle-sharp talons and flies back to his perch. He stores his catch in a fork of the tree, where it quickly freezes in the wintry air.

Nearby, the owl's mate snuggles down over her two eggs, keeping them warm and safe. She can't leave the nest when she is hungry, so her mate will feed her. Since the mouse is frozen like an ice cube, the male owl has to melt it somehow. He sits on the mouse, and the warmth of his body thaws it. Now he can give his mate a delicious defrosted treat.

PILED HIGH

It's harvest time! A pika scurries by with a mouthful of fresh grass. He tosses his bundle onto a big stack of shoots and grasses, and then disappears to find more. All day long the pika adds to his tall haystack. Among the green and brown stems and leaves are bright flowers — the blossoms of yellow alpine arnica, Red Indian Paintbrush and blue harebells.

The pika's haystack is already as big as the huge boulders on the mountain slope. Sometimes he spreads grass on the rocks to dry in the late summer sun before moving it to his pile. Why? Like a farmer, he knows the sun-dried food will keep well over the winter months.

Through the winter, the pika will search for lichens, bark and roots in the snow. But when a winter storm blows in, this wise little mountain animal can feed on the plants he piled high for those blustery days.

HIDE AND SEEK

Chickadee-dee-dee! The chickadee chirps her name as she hunts for food, even after she has eaten. She finds a tiny seed and flies off with it cupped in her beak. She tucks this treasure into the crevice of a tree. She hides another seed in a hollow stem nearby. She finds and hides seed after seed. Such an active little bird will need all these small meals later.

Will the chickadee be able to find all her secret hiding spots? When she returns, she suddenly darts towards the tree crevice. The seed is right there! The chickadee flits from hiding place to hiding place, finding every hidden seed. She remembers the way the hiding spots look and returns to them one by one.

In northern areas, chickadees hide seeds in the fall to eat during the winter. Weeks after hiding their food, these little birds remember where it is hidden . . . even if a snowfall has blanketed the trees and changed the autumn forest to winter white!

SOAKING WET

Two bulging eyes and a round snout poke out of the murky river. A crocodile is floating just below the surface of the water like a bumpy old log. Silent and still, he watches a thirsty water buffalo come to the river's edge. When it bends down to lap some water, Snap! The crocodile's jaws open and close like giant scissors. He pulls his dinner into the river.

The crocodile is hungry, but he has to wait. His long, sharp teeth are good for grasping but not as good for chewing. The tough meat has to soften in the water before he can eat it. The crocodile drags his meal to a hole in the muddy river bank. It is the perfect place to keep the food for a few days until it is nice and tender. The water will hide the meat from the vultures. It will wash away the smell that would bring other animals to steal his dinner. Patiently, the crocodile floats nearby, waiting for his feast.

A Sweet Team

Bzzzzzzzz, Bzzzzzzzz! Honeybees burst into the hive with the good news. Pollen and nectar! But in which direction? How far away? The bees start to dance and their hive mates crowd around. Bees who have found new flowers full of food dance this special waggle dance. It tells other bees where to collect the pollen and nectar to bring back to the hive.

The hive is home to the whole colony. This is where the bees keep the food they gather. All the honeybees work together to keep their honey safe and fresh.

After worker bees have collected nectar, other bees in the hive dry the nectar into honey. To keep it from spoiling, they mix in preservatives they make in their bodies. Then they store the honey in honeycombs. Guard bees buzz around outside. They attack and sting any stranger, from the smallest ant to the biggest bear, that tries to steal the sweet honey from the hive.

WOOD FOR WINTER

Back and forth the beavers swim, dragging branches and twigs in their mouths. This family has work to finish before winter comes. They use their large front teeth to cut down trees, gnawing and chopping. Stick by stick, they build their house, or lodge, from the tougher branches. They will live all winter in their lodge, right in the middle of the frozen pond covered with snow.

The beavers save the tenderest branches for their winter food supply. They store tasty twigs inside the warm, dry lodge. They pile more food in a huge underwater mound, jamming big branches into the muddy pond bottom and stuffing smaller twigs in between. The pile grows until it reaches all the way to the surface of the pond. When the pond freezes over, the best pieces will be beneath the ice, easy to pull out and drag home.

All through the winter, the beaver family will munch on the food they've collected. When all the twigs in their lodge are gone, the beavers will swim under the frozen surface of the pond to the big pile of food just outside their door! Just like carrot sticks sitting in water in your fridge, the twigs stay juicy and crisp in the icy cold pond.

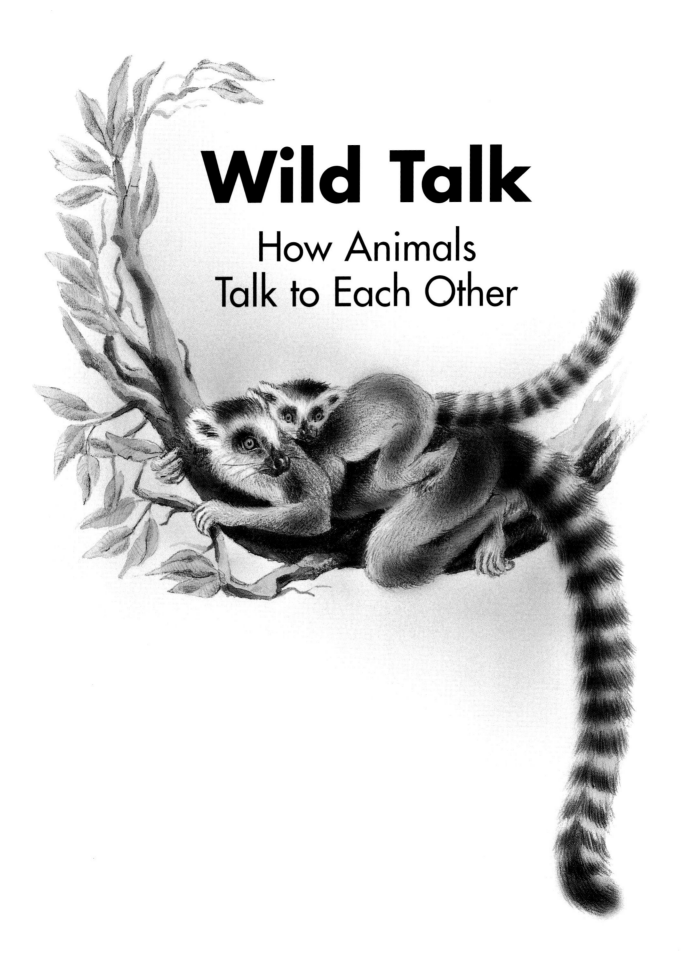

Wild Talk

How Animals
Talk to Each Other

ANIMAL TALK

How do you talk to other people? You can speak, shout, whisper or use hand signals to get your message across. You can smile or frown, or hug someone to let them know how you feel. You can teach someone something by showing them what to do. People understand by watching and listening to you. Animals have a lot to say to each other, too. They don't use words. They use special signals and signs for other animals to see, hear, smell or feel.

How do animals talk to each other? To find mates, tiny fireflies signal with light and cranes dance. To feel close to others in their families, elephants rumble and chimpanzees touch. Howler monkeys roar and ring-tailed lemurs leave their scent to keep others away. Great frigate birds do things over and over again to teach their young how to act. Humpback whales sing, but no one is exactly sure why.

Wolves sometimes "speak" with the looks on their faces and the way they sit or stand. From the time they are very young, baby wolves watch their parents and then copy their actions while they play. Look carefully at the wolf pups playing in this picture. Can you tell which one is acting angry, which one is acting hungry, which one feels left out and which one wants to play? Now turn the pages and let some animals talk to you.

HIGH-UP HOWLING

A roar jolts the sleeping rain forest just as the sun comes up. "Aaarrooo-oo-oo-gaaahhh!" A howler monkey greets the day with his booming howl. Soon, all the howler monkeys in the troop join in the leader's noisy call. The big voice box in the throat of a howler monkey makes deep, loud roars. The males have the largest voice boxes and the deepest calls.

One by one, the males, females and babies follow the leader as he moves through the treetops. In a long line they search for figs, flowers or nuts to eat. But look, there are other howler monkeys nearby! The howlers start roaring again. "Get away!" they seem to say, "You can't have the food from our trees." All day they guard their part of the forest from the other howler monkeys. And, when the sun goes down, they all roar together once more before going to sleep high in the treetops.

DANCE WITH ME

Two Japanese cranes, a male and a female, greet each other. They face each other and start to dance, casting swaying shadows on the snow. As their graceful wings unfold, they bend and bow. Suddenly, the male springs up into the air. Up, up, again and again he jumps. The female watches him and dances around him. Then it's her turn to dance as he watches.

Soon other cranes in the flock find partners and begin to dance, too. The wintering ground is full of dancing cranes. These birds dance to find a mate for life. Together a pair of cranes will hatch eggs into chicks. They will move to other places as the seasons change. They will dance together many times to show how close they are. But this first time, they dance their very best.

SMELLY SIGNALS

A troop of ring-tailed lemurs stops to rest. They touch and clean each other's fur. Sometimes they make soft grunting noises. This is how they say that they all belong together. After a warm bask in the sun, they start to move through the dry Madagascan forest. They hold their long striped tails straight up as they travel. One female lemur leads them as they search for food.

Suddenly the leader stops and does a hand-stand. She brushes her bottom against a low tree branch. As the base of her tail touches the branch, it leaves a smell there. It's a message to other lemur troops that this part of the forest is taken. Each lemur in the troop flips upside-down to leave a message too. But sometimes lemurs from other troops still get too close. Then the males stand up on their hind legs and rub their tails over scent glands on their wrists. Their tails get loaded with smelly musk. On four feet, they move towards the strangers. They quickly flick their tails, sending a smelly warning. Peee-uuu!

NIGHT LIGHTS

Blink, blink . . . flash! A male firefly darts through the warm evening air. He lights up again and again, like a tiny flashlight flicking on and off. His signal is seen by the female fireflies in the grass. Flash! A female lights up at the right time to catch his attention. He zigzags in her direction. Their lights tell each other that they are the same kind of firefly, so they will be perfect mates.

Fireflies carry a built-in lantern in their bodies. The cold, greenish glow is made by special chemicals inside the firefly. Each kind of firefly has its own special code. The code is made up of flashes of light, quick and slow, bright and dim. That's how a hungry female firefly can fool a male of another kind of firefly. She blinks back his signal and waits for him to fly down. Then, to his surprise, he becomes a meal instead of a mate. Blink, blink . . . glub!

WARNING WHINNY

Zebras peacefully munch on grasses, side by side with
antelopes. There is safety in numbers for all the animals.
"Ee-aa, ee-aa," a zebra mare neighs softly to keep in
touch with her foal. Zebras know each other by voice,
stripe pattern and scent. They sniff the breeze for the
smell of danger. Suddenly, their ears twitch forward and
their nostrils quiver. They are on the alert.

A lioness is creeping through the long grass. A large zebra stallion barks a loud warning, "Danger! Gallop away!" In the dust of stamping hooves, zebra families come together. A mare leads the escape. The foals and other mares in her family follow. The strong stallion protects from the back of the group. A mass of black and white stripes streaks across the African plains to safety.

LEADER OF THE PACK

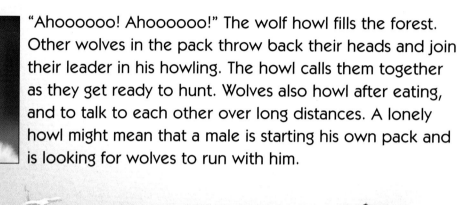

"Ahoooooo! Ahoooooo!" The wolf howl fills the forest. Other wolves in the pack throw back their heads and join their leader in his howling. The howl calls them together as they get ready to hunt. Wolves also howl after eating, and to talk to each other over long distances. A lonely howl might mean that a male is starting his own pack and is looking for wolves to run with him.

Each wolf has a special place in the wolf pack. All the wolves obey the leader. He holds his tail high and fluffs out his fur to tell the others that he is in command. Another wolf flattens his ears and tucks in his tail, whines and licks the leader's muzzle, signalling, "You are our chief." And if the wolves forget who is in charge, the leader reminds them with a glare, an angry face and bared teeth. The pups in the pack watch carefully. Their parents teach them by example, so they will learn their place in the pack.

As the wolves move through the woods, they leave urine markings on trees. The smell tells other wolves who has been here and how long ago. Wolves mark all around their territory to keep other wolf packs away. The pack will need all the food in this area to survive.

SEEING RED

Is that a bright red balloon in the branches? No, it's a male great frigate bird. He has a colorful way to signal that he is looking for a mate. His fire-red throat pouch puffs out, shining in the Galapagos sun. He shows off, flapping his wings and clacking his bill. Finally, a female arrives to be his partner. They build a nest of twigs and hatch one white egg into a chick.

Great frigate birds are fantastic fliers. Fast and smooth, they dip and soar in the air. The parents must teach their chick how to hunt on the wing, so both parents show the chick over and over again. First they show it how to swoop down on sticks and feathers. Once the chick can grab floating sticks from the air, it tries for fish near the surface of the ocean. Great frigate birds cannot dive into the sea to catch fish, so the chick must learn to get close to the food on the top of the water. Its parents teach it to fly so well, it can even snatch food on the wing from other birds.

DEEP SEA SONGS

Deep groans and high whistles, loud roars and soft sighs — the ocean is full of whale music. The songs of the humpback whales echo through the water. "Sigh . . . squawk, chirp, groan . . . roar!" Male humpbacks swim in a group. Each whale sings almost the same song, and their voices flow together. As they chant, their song changes during the long voyage. From the cold Arctic ocean they glide to warm breeding waters. They sing the most here, where the humpback cows and calves gather.

What messages are the whales sending? Nobody really knows. The male whales sing near the females. Are they singing for a mate? The humpbacks sing on long swims through the ocean. Are they telling other whales where they are? Are they warning away others from where they feed? There is so much more for us to learn about these singing giants.

CHIMP CHATTER

Two young chimpanzees play on the forest floor, rolling and tickling. When the baby flops into their mother's lap, she holds and strokes him. He whimpers and pouts at his big sister, who pats at his back and snuggles beside him. The mother chimpanzee gently cleans her children's fur. The family uses play and touching and sound to say how close they feel.

Other chimpanzees appear through the leafy bushes. Their soft cries of pleasure and excited faces show they are friends. Both these families belong to the same chimpanzee group. Chimpanzees in the group talk to each other in many ways. They loudly call and hoot to keep in touch over long distances. Their faces show if they are angry, happy, afraid or surprised. Their hands reach out to ask for something, to make friends, or to shoo another chimpanzee away. The adults in the group protect this area of the forest. If outsiders come too close, they run at them with their arms stretched high and bark an angry "Wraa!"

SERENADE IN BLUE

"Chur-wi, chur-wi, chur-wi," the bluebird warbles from the top of a fence. He has shed his old feathers, and his new ones shimmer in the morning sun. His mate admires his sky-blue feathers and his lilting love song. He flies across the spring green field to her, carrying a juicy grasshopper as a gift. He feeds it to her to let her know that it's time to build a nest and lay eggs.

Soon the eggs hatch into hungry nestlings. The bright yellow of their gaping mouths tells the parents what the babies want. "Feed me, feed me!" they squawk and chirp. Their parents take turns feeding the chicks. They fly far to find insects for the young to eat. At last the father bluebird rests on a branch outside his home. "Chur-wi, chur-wi, chur-wi," he calls. He tells the other birds that this is where his family is, so stay away.

LONG DISTANCE CALL

Trekking across the African plain, a herd of elephants stops suddenly. The female elephants and calves that make up the herd stand very still. They all face the same direction, and lift their large ears to listen. There isn't a sound to be heard by you or me. But the elephants are getting a deep, rumbling message from far away. It's another elephant herd, travelling in the same direction.

The elephants answer with the same rumbling sounds from the base of their trunks. The rumbles are loud and travel a long way. But they are too deep for human ears to hear. Groups of elephants use the rumbles to keep in touch as they travel. Males and females also rumble to each other across vast distances. When a female is ready to mate, she sends a message far and wide. Male elephants, roaming alone, hear her and know where to find her. They follow her call and fight for her attention.

Elephants have many other ways of talking to each other. They snort, trumpet, touch trunks and turn in circles. By smell and touch and sound, they greet each other and stay close in their groups. But for long-distance messages, elephants use the deep, low rumbling to talk across the plains.

FROGGY EVENING

All through the day, the bullfrog floats in the water near the edge of the pond. Once in a while, he catches a dragonfly with his swift tongue. Without a sound, he waits for night to fall. When tall bullrushes and reeds finally cast moon shadows on the pond, he starts to sing in a great, booming voice. "Aurumph, aurumph, aurumph," he croaks into the cool spring night.

After a silent winter, why is the bullfrog singing now? When the spring sun makes the pond water warm enough, the bullfrog knows it's time to find a mate. He forces air past his windpipe to make a croak. A sac of loose skin at his throat starts to puff out like a balloon. The sound will echo in this sac and boom past the pond and over the meadow. He is announcing to the world that he is looking for a female. He tells other males that this is his area in the pond, so stay out. If a female bullfrog likes his song, they will mate. Soon the bullfrog will be silent again, and the pond will be full of baby frogs called tadpoles.

Who's Who

GIANT TORTOISE AND DARWIN'S GROUND FINCH

The giant tortoise and Darwin's ground finch live on the Galapagos Islands. The tortoise can grow during its whole long life to reach the size of a bathtub. The ground finch is about the size of your fist. It was named for Charles Darwin, who studied many animals found only on the Galapagos.

ANTS AND APHIDS

Ants live almost everywhere in the world except cold polar areas. In their groups, called colonies, work is shared and each ant has a special job. Aphids are green and about the size of the lead poking out of a pencil. Because they suck juices out of plants, they are pests in gardens.

SQUIRREL MONKEY

Capuchin monkeys and squirrel monkeys live in South American forests. Squirrel monkeys are like squirrels in their size and because they use their long tails for balance as they climb and jump. Capuchins are about the size of large cats, and usually stay high in the tops of the rain forest trees.

RHINOCEROS AND CATTLE EGRETS

Rhinoceroses are found in dry bush and scrub areas in Africa. An adult rhino is about the size of a small car. Cattle egrets are originally from Africa, but have spread to North and South America and even Australia. A cattle egret would be a little taller than the seat of a chair.

BLUE SHARK

Sharks come in many shapes and sizes. But all have many rows of sharp teeth they use to tear at the food they find in the coastal seas where they swim. Remoras are fish that live in tropical and temperate seas. A remora can be as long as your hand or even longer than your arm.

THREE-TOED SLOTH

The three-toed sloth lives in the rain forests of Central and South America. Its body is about the size of a big cat, but its arms are very long so it can hang from trees. More than a hundred sloth moths might live on one sloth. Each dull brown moth is about the length of your thumbnail.

CLOWN FISH AND SEA ANEMONE

Clown fish swim in warm, shallow ocean waters, especially the Red Sea and the Indo-Pacific Ocean. A clown fish is about the size of your hand held flat. Sea anemones come in many sizes and bright colors. They can be as small as a toothbrush or as big as a bush, and their tentacles can be long and feathery or short and stubby.

GIRAFFE AND ZEBRA

Giraffes, gerenuks, Thomson's gazelles and zebras all live on the plains of East Africa. The giraffe is the tallest animal in the world. Zebras are just like striped horses. The gerenuk is about the size of a goat, and is sometimes called the giraffe-gazelle because of its long neck. The delicate Thomson's gazelles are smaller still.

BLACK-TAILED PRAIRIE DOG

Home for black-tailed prairie dogs is the North American plains. They dig tunnels and burrows to make whole towns underground. A prairie dog is the size of a very small dog. Burrowing owls also live on the North American prairie. They are about the size of robins, and hunt during the day and evening.

CLEANER WRASSE AND GROUPER

Cleaner wrasse fish set up cleaning stations in corral reefs, alone or in groups of two or three. A wrasse is about the length of a grown-up's finger. Butterflyfish and angelfish live in tropical waters in the Indo-Pacific. Butterflyfish are only about as long as your hand, but angelfish can be as long as a grown-up's arm.

TUATARA

Tuataras are lizard-like reptiles that live only on the islands off the coast of New Zealand. A tuatara is only about as long as your arm, but it is related to dinosaurs. Diving petrels are about the size of seagulls, and they fish the seas of the southern hemisphere. They gather in large groups to nest in holes in the rocks of cliffs overlooking the sea.

RATEL

Ratels are a little bigger than skunks, with the same black and white fur and long claws for digging. Also called honey badgers, they live in Africa, Asia and India. The honeyguide bird lives near forests in East and Central Africa. It is small enough to fit on the palm of your hand. People, as well as ratels, follow the honeyguide to find honey.

ASIAN ELEPHANT

Elephants are the largest land animals, and live in forested and open areas of Africa and Asia. At birth, a baby elephant stands about as tall as a three-year-old child and weighs as much as a large man. Many wild elephants have been hunted and killed just for their ivory tusks.

SEA OTTER

All wild sea otters live in the Pacific Ocean, swimming and floating off the coasts of North America and northern Asia. They can be as big as large dogs, with cubs the size of puppies. Sea otters keep the kelp beds healthy by eating sea urchins, since too many sea urchins would eat up all the kelp.

RED KANGAROO

Kangaroos are pouched mammals, or marsupials. They live in Australia, Tasmania and New Guinea. Kangaroos come in various sizes, but the red kangaroo is the largest, almost as tall as a human. A new-born kangaroo is the size of a bumblebee when it crawls into its mother's pouch.

LITTLE BROWN BAT

Of all mammals, only bats can truly fly. They live in most tropical and temperate areas of the world. Little brown bats eat insects, but some bats eat fruit, and a few even drink blood. The little brown bat's body is smaller than your palm, and its babies at birth are the size of plum pits.

RED-BILLED HORNBILL

Red-billed hornbills nest in East and Central Africa, in dry bush and open woodland areas. Other kinds of hornbills live in Africa and in tropical Asia, and most of them plaster up their nesting holes, too. The mother hornbill stays sealed up in the nest for about a month until her eggs hatch.

AMERICAN ALLIGATOR

You'll find the American alligator living in marsh-lands in the southern part of North America. A newly hatched baby alligator is the size of a telephone receiver. In six to ten years, it will grow as long as a man is tall, and as an adult it can keep growing to become more than twice that size.

EMPEROR PENGUIN

Penguins are birds but they cannot fly, except underwater where they are excellent swimmers. On land, they sometimes toboggan on their bellies over the ice and snow of the Antarctic. The emperor is the biggest penguin, and its head can reach as high as the hood of a car. At birth a fluffy penguin chick is as tall as a brand new pencil.

MEERKAT

Meerkats or dwarf mongooses live in small colonies in the dry areas of eastern and southern Africa. They are the size of rabbits only slimmer, and their babies are about the size of mice. When the adults are out hunting for insects and small reptiles, the one that is assigned guard duty stays behind and watches for danger.

ORANGUTAN

Humans are cutting down the tropical forests where they live, so the orangutans that are left today are found only in Borneo and northern Sumatra. Males live alone and females travel with their young. A newborn orangutan is about the size of a kitten and is as helpless as a newborn human baby.

POLAR BEAR

Home for polar bears is the frozen Arctic. Polar bear babies are often born as twins, each about the size of a guinea pig. Cubs spend their first two winters with their mother under the snow. A hunting polar bear might cover its shiny black nose with a white paw, making itself almost invisible against the ice.

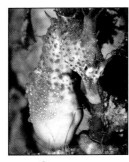

SEAHORSE

Seahorses live in the shallow, inland waters of Indo-Australia. They are also found in the Atlantic and Pacific Oceans. Newborns are only about the size of your thumbnail, but are born ready to find food and swim. Many fish fathers care for their young, but it's only the seahorse father that actually gets pregnant with the babies.

CUCKOO

Cuckoos live in many parts of the world, including Europe and North America. Nearly half lay eggs in the nests of other birds. Cuckoo chicks quickly grow big, sometimes bigger than their foster parents. Some cuckoo chicks shove out of the nest anything that touches their back, making more room and getting more food for themselves.

KANGAROO RAT

Kangaroo rats live in dry scrub and desert areas through North, Central and northern South America. The kangaroo rat is a bit bigger than a mouse. Its oversized back legs and a tail that is three times the length of its body give it the strength and balance to jump several times its own height.

MacGREGOR'S BOWERBIRD

Most bowerbirds live in northern Australia, but MacGregor's bowerbird lives in the lush mountain forests of New Guinea. It is about the same size as a North American robin. Each bowerbird has its own unique bower design to attract females and sometimes to display food and treasures.

ACORN WOODPECKER

Acorn woodpeckers live in large family groups in the wooded foothills and mixed forests of southwestern North America, and further south into the tropics. The length of your forearm from your elbow to your wrist is about how high an acorn woodpecker would stand.

LEOPARD

Leopards live in the rainforests, deserts, mountains or lowland plains of Asia and Africa. Now only a few leopards are left since they have been hunted for their beautiful spotted fur. A leopard is about the size of a big dog, but is muscular, very sleek, and extremely powerful.

GARDEN SPIDER

Garden spiders live worldwide except in Antarctica. Not all kinds of spiders spin webs, but garden spiders are part of the large group that do. Look among plants and you might recognize a web and a waiting spider with thread-thin legs and a body about the size of the tip of your thumb.

HONEYPOT ANTS

Honeypot ants live in dry areas of Australia, North America and Africa. Underground nests are divided into "galleries": nurseries near the surface where it is warm, and food stores deeper where it is cool. Repletes, or storage ants, swell from the size of a grain of sand to the size of a pea.

GREAT HORNED OWL

Great horned owls live in the wooded and open areas of North, Central and South America. They often hatch their eggs in nests that have been built and abandoned by other birds. Listen for a low "Hoot, hoot, hoot, hoot," and look for a large bird with wings that open about as far as an adult's out-stretched arms.

CROCODILE

Crocodiles live in the rivers, lakes and swamps of tropical regions all over the world. The ancestors of today's crocodiles lived at the time of the dinosaurs and were about the length of a school bus. Now crocodiles are only car-length but, like their relatives, they have huge, powerful jaws that can snap shut like a steel trap.

PIKA

In grassy nests cradled between the rocks, pikas live in the Rocky Mountains of western North America and in mountains throughout Asia. If you see one, it will be a furry animal the size of a small guinea pig scurrying amongst the boulders or running on top of the snow. If you hear a short, sharp whistle, you'll know that it's a pika.

HONEYBEE

Wild honeybees build nests in holes of trees or in rocky openings in temperate and tropical regions of Europe, Asia, North America and Africa. People through-out the world keep honeybees for the use of their delicious honey. If you see a honeybee buzz by, it will be about the size of the metal eraser-holder on the end of a pencil.

CHICKADEE

Chickadees are friendly, living in wooded back-yards, parks and forests of North America. Listen for a cheery "chick-a-dee-dee-dee" call and look for a small bird about the size of a child's fist. Expect more than one, since they live in pairs through spring and summer, and start to gather into small flocks in August.

BEAVER

Beavers live in streams, ponds and lakes in the cooler parts of North America and Asia. The beaver is the size of a small dog, with a broad, flat tail and two long, orange front teeth. In the winter, if you pass a lodge of sticks in the middle of a frozen pond, you just might hear the soft sounds of the beavers inside.

RED HOWLER MONKEY

Howler monkeys live in tropical forests and range from southern Mexico through Central America, to northern Argentina in South America. They can have red, black or brown fur, and they all use their prehensile tails to cling to branches. They are the size of a medium-sized dog.

FIREFLY

Fireflies live in woods and meadows, near streams and even in back yards. There are more than 130 species or types of fireflies around the world, each with its own light code. A firefly is a bit longer than a housefly, but all you would notice is a quick, bright flash if you saw one at night.

JAPANESE CRANE

Japanese or Manchurian cranes are a symbol of love, happiness and long life in Japan. Their graceful shapes are used on clothing and artwork. They are the largest cranes in Japan and live on the northern island of Hokkaido. Tall and elegant, they are about the height of a twelve-year-old child.

ZEBRA

A zebra looks like a horse with black and white stripes. There are three kinds of zebras, and they all live in Africa. Although all zebras have stripes, no two zebras have exactly the same stripe pattern. Zebras are often found in mixed herds along with antelopes or wildebeest.

RING-TAILED LEMUR

All lemurs live in Madagascar, off the coast of Africa. Ring-tailed lemurs live in the dry southern forests of this big island. During the day, they travel in troops of up to 25, and at night they curl up together to keep warm. An adult is the size of a large housecat, but has a much longer tail.

WOLF

Wolves are related to dogs, but are bigger and have longer legs. Gray or Timber wolves can range in color from black to white. They live in packs in northern North America and Eurasia, preferring open forests and tundra. The leader of the pack and his mate are called the alpha male and female.

GREAT FRIGATE BIRD

Frigate birds nest on tropical islands, such as the Galapagos Islands off the coast of South America. Their wide wingspans and light bodies make these sea birds agile fliers. They can even steal food from other birds in midair. A frigate bird's wingspan is about as far as you and a friend could stretch out your arms side by side.

EASTERN BLUEBIRD

Look in orchards and open farmland in North America and you might see a bluebird. The Eastern bluebird is a little longer than your outstretched hand, and is bright blue with an orangey chest. Some bluebirds' natural nesting sites were taken over by house sparrows and starlings, so people have set up nest boxes for them to use.

HUMPBACK WHALE

Humpback whales migrate through the oceans from the polar waters to the tropical seas. They are huge but agile, leaping out of the waves and slapping the surface of the water with their wide tails as they dive back in. A humpback whale is about as long as two school buses parked end to end.

AFRICAN ELEPHANT

You can find African elephants in the forest and open savannah areas of Africa. The low, rumbling sound that they send over long distances comes from the area where their trunks meet their foreheads. It is called infrasound. Infrasound is also in wind, thunder and ocean storms, but we can't hear it.

CHIMPANZEE

Chimpanzees are found throughout west, central and east Africa, wherever there are rain forests, mountain forests and savannah woodlands. Just like humans, chimpanzees show various facial expressions, and they are our closest living animal relatives. An adult chimpanzee is just a little shorter than the average human.

BULLFROG

Home for the American bullfrog is in the lakes and ponds of North America. It is the largest species of frog in North America, and has the loudest croak. An adult bullfrog with its legs outstretched is about the length of a tall drinking glass. When fully inflated, the male's throat sac can be half again as big as the whole frog.

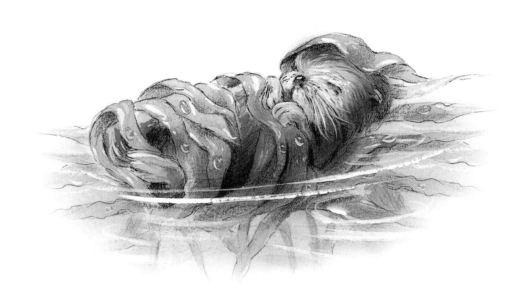